"Too many Americans face a dismal future because they failed to truly plan for the longest vacation of their lives—*retirement*. People continue to live longer lives. They face a double-headed monster, the twin predators of wealth known as taxes and inflation. Just as important is their *purpose* during their retirement years. *Fish Don't Clap* addresses these issues and more!"

— Michael Roby, Financial Industry Speaker,
Coach, and Consultant

FISH
DON'T
CLAP

FISH DON'T CLAP

Planning for a Purposeful Retirement

BRAD CONNORS, CWS®

Foreword by Don Connelly

For more information contact:
iWealth
213 15th Ave NE.
Waseca, MN 56093
www.iWealth4me.com

ISBN: 978-0-692-32274-1 – paperback
ISBN: 978-0-692-32273-4 – e-Book

Library of Congress Control Number: 2014955497

Securities, advisory services, and insurance products are offered through Investment Centers of America, Inc. (ICA), member FINRA, SIPC, a Registered Investment Advisor, and affiliated insurance agencies. ICA and iWealth are separate companies.

All investing involves risks, including the possible loss of principal amount invested, and there is no guarantee that your investment objectives will be met. No investment strategy guarantees future success.

The tax and legal information presented in this material is general in nature and should not be construed as tax or legal advice. Neither ICA, nor its representatives provide tax or legal advice.

Please consult your tax and/or legal advisor for guidance regarding your particular situation before making any changes.

The scenarios presented in this material are hypothetical in nature and are not intended to portray any past or future events and your own experience may vary.

*Pages 28 & 71: The R-Factor Question® is a registered trademark, protected by copyright and an integral concept owned by The Strategic Coach® Inc. All rights reserved. Used with written permission. www.strategiccoach.com.

This book was written with technical assistance from BusinessGhost, Inc.

*By the grace of God,
thank you to my loving family,
mentors, and team.
Thank you for all you do!*

C O N T E N T S

Contents

THERE ARE SEVERAL reasons why someone who is planning for the future might want to read what Brad Connors has to say. The most important reason is that it will get you thinking about yourself—not just about your financial well-being, but about your personal happiness.

Very rarely, if ever, have you ever done anything for the first time and gotten it right. And when you finally retire, it will be for the first time. There will be no do-overs. You've got to get it right. I am telling you now that you don't retire on a lump sum of money; you retire on the income from a lump sum of money. Anybody can manage a lump sum of money. You can bury it in the back yard if you want to. But it takes a pro to manage income.

This book is about writing down everything on your bucket list and figuring out how much each activity costs.

Brad's advice is to decide what you want to do and work backwards. That one big vacation a year is a lot more fun if you are spending interest and not principal.

I read *Fish Don't Clap* with a great deal of interest. Like Brad's protagonist, Hal, I am a public speaker. Because I live in Florida, I have over twenty years' experience observing retirees who have relocated from the Midwest and Canada. Many are without a compass—they retired without definitive plans, apart from a vague expectation of good weather and golf courses. They drift into a routine—one day becomes the next, which becomes the next. Their relevance begins to fade, and the phone calls from their former colleagues stop. They transition from doers to consumers, and many don't feel vital anymore—being on a condo board is not terribly fulfilling. If they don't have enough money to do things, they begin to lose their dignity. I don't want to end up like that, and neither do you.

Others retire with gusto and have a ball. They don't fade into retirement; they jump into retirement. They know what they want to do, and they know they can afford to do it. They don't feel guilty about spending money, and they don't live in fear of outliving their money. In other words, they have a plan and the plan works.

If you read *Fish Don't Clap*, you will want the kind of plan Hal has in the end. You'll list your dreams and you'll figure out, dream by dream, what you can afford to do and what you can't afford to do. In other words, you'll have a plan that works. You'll make tough decisions that serve you well for the rest of your life.

You and your family are the most important people you know. If you don't take care of yourselves, no one else will. I assure you that of all the buckets from which you draw money—Social Security, 401(k), et cetera—the biggest single bucket will be your personal savings. You will not be retiring from the company store. You'll be retiring to the business of running your own retirement company. If you don't know how to run a retirement company, you need to hire a pro to do it for you. Don't do it alone, and don't do it without an all-weather plan.

If you retire at age sixty-five and live to be ninety, prices will probably triple during those years. Your income won't. Worry about that now, not when you're sixty-five. Read this book and hire a pro. Don't think you can plan your retirement on your own. A guide is a lot more valuable than a compass and a map.

The weather's great. Come on down. Just make sure you have enough money to do what you want.

Don Connelly
President, Don Connelly and Associates

CHAPTER ONE

Fish Don't Clap

HAL SAT DRUMMING his fingers against the metal rim of his fishing boat. It was a little after sunrise on a Tuesday, and he was out in the middle of a small, crystal-blue mountain lake. Over the tree line, the sky still held traces of the astonishing blend of orange and pink left by the sunrise minutes before.

Aside from the soft cadence of Hal's fingers against the boat, the morning was virtually silent. Every few minutes, a burst of birdsong came up from the dense foliage on the lakeshore, or the wind gently rustled branches hanging out over the lake. But mostly the forest was motionless and still. Hal was the center of a serene universe.

Tap. Tap, tap.

Hal drummed his fingers. Impulsively, he reached over and gave his fishing line a quick tug. Nothing. The line was slack.

Tap, tap, tap.

Unconsciously, Hal let out a long, drawn-out sigh. He tested the line again. And then he drew his hand back, puzzled.

What was he doing? He was an experienced enough fisherman to know better than to agitate his line and make useless noise against the side of his boat. Why was he fidgeting so much? Why couldn't he just relax?

"I'm bored," Hal realized, the answer to his unspoken questions coming to him in a flash. But as soon as this thought arose, Hal shook his head, pushing it away.

Bored? Impossible. This was only the third fishing trip he'd taken since retiring six months before—and fishing was what he had looked forward to the most after wrapping up his career. Hal had been working as a public speaker for thirty-five fruitful, happy years. He primarily worked with top-level executives at Fortune 500 and 1000 companies, conducting workshops that not only helped people get energized around a common goal but also guided them through serious introspection that helped them to realize their potential. It was extremely rewarding work but also extremely strenuous—mentally and sometimes even physically.

Hal had always managed his speaking engagements

himself, and as an entrepreneur, he had always been very diligent in planning for retirement. It was a goal he'd kept in mind throughout his career, thoughtfully setting aside money and curbing his expenditures. And when, at sixty-eight, his financial advisor had let him know that his retirement account had reached the benchmark the two of them had determined, Hal had leapt into retirement without a second thought. He couldn't have been more thrilled to have the time for exactly this kind of fishing trip.

All right, I'm definitely not bored, Hal thought to himself, shifting his weight and placing his booted feet on the empty bench across from him. But if he was not bored, what was he? Anxious?

Hal scanned his mind. Could he have forgotten something important, left something undone before he had "gone fishin'"? But what was there on a retiree's to-do list? His wife was safe at home with plenty of friends and volunteer work to keep her busy in his absence; the bills were paid; his various insurance policies were in order; his two kids were both employed and each standing on their own two feet.

Hal shifted again. There was nothing to be anxious about, and yet he was restless. Where was that gentle stillness that usually descended on him when he was out on the water? Ordinarily the deep quiet of the woods would lull him into a sense of ease and oneness with the world, but today the silence felt deafening. Uncomfortable. Nagging.

Just then, Hal's line pulled taut. He sprang into action, his movements quick and sure. A lifetime of fishing had made him skilled and deft; he reeled in a big, fat trout without having to think twice. He pulled the fish into the boat and held it aloft, watching the water gleam on its blue-gray scales, one small, black eye staring widely at him, its gills still subtly swaying open and shut, open and shut.

Just then, a thought leapt into his mind.

Fish don't clap.

• • •

"I'm a public speaker," Hal was saying to the slightly younger man who had just taken a seat next to him at the hunting lodge where he was staying. It was midmorning, and after catching his trout he'd decided to cut that day's fishing expedition short. The small café at the lodge was packed with end-of-summer vacationers who were just coming in for breakfast, and Hal had found himself sharing a table. The younger man had introduced himself as Richard, a consultant who was taking a long weekend to hike around the surrounding mountainside. They discovered quickly that they were both from the same small city, a few hours' drive from the lodge, and the conversation unfolded from there.

"Well, I *was* a public speaker," Hal corrected himself. "I retired about six months ago."

"Congratulations!" Richard said. "That's fantastic."

Hal furrowed his brow. Richard had an easy, relaxed manner. Maybe because of this, or maybe just because of being out in the wilderness, away from the usual social constraints, Hal found himself saying, "I'm not so sure. I thought it would be—fantastic, I mean—but . . . how can I put this?"

He paused. Despite having spent an entire career on the public speaking circuit, sometimes speaking before audiences of hundreds of people two or three times a day, he wasn't given to many words in his private life. He preferred to let his actions speak for themselves.

"I'm suddenly feeling—and I can hardly believe I'm saying this—like retirement isn't all it's cracked up to be," Hal said. "This morning the strangest thing happened."

Hal was still a little surprised to hear himself saying all this to a complete stranger, but Richard looked interested, and so he went on. "For the first time in my life, I was sitting there in my fishing boat, and I thought, *There's got to be more to it than this.* As it turns out, I think retirement might actually be kind of boring."

Richard threw back his head and let out a long, hearty laugh. Hal couldn't help himself; he had to join in.

"I know! It's crazy; isn't it?" Hal exclaimed. "I mean, basically my whole life has been leading up to this . . . and now that I'm here, I'm thinking, *What's next?* But there isn't any 'next'! This is the end of the line."

Richard sobered up a bit, taking a swig from his mug of hot coffee. "Wow," he said. "When you put it that way . . . well, it gives you pause, doesn't it? I mean, here I am on my yearly trip thinking, *Won't it be great when I can do this any time I want to, for as long as I want to?* And you're sitting on the other side of the finish line, telling me maybe I'm not aiming in the right direction."

Hal chuckled. "Don't get me wrong. I'm not saying I want to go back to work. I was traveling two or three days out of the week, taking on as many gigs as I could to fill my calendar, sometimes running my voice ragged. I wouldn't want to spend the rest of my life doing that. I don't think I'd be physically able to, even if I wanted to. But I got this strange feeling of nostalgia this morning," he continued. "And when I asked myself why, it suddenly came to me. *Fish don't clap.* I've spent my whole life inspiring people to take control of their lives, to start creating the results they envision for themselves by tapping into their potential and truly realizing a life of happiness . . . and now all of a sudden I'm sitting in a boat all alone on a lake, and I miss that feeling of having a real purpose. Of having a job to do every day and knowing right away, in the moment, whether I've done it well or not. Because an audience will let you know. They either clap or they don't.

"It's an almost uncanny feeling," Hal continued. "I spent my career talking about purpose and passion and drive . . . and now *I'm* the one who feels unmoored and directionless."

Richard nodded slowly. "But if you don't want to go back to the speaking circuit and you don't want to be out here, performing for the fishes . . . what's left?"

"That's exactly the question," Hal agreed. "And I can't believe I never thought to ask it before."

"I can't believe I didn't either," Richard said. "You're suddenly making me realize that I've been on autopilot, in a way. You know what I mean? We sort of get on a track and start moving forward: You go to school, start a career, start a family, and then you start building toward retirement. Build up a retirement account, shore up your life, and then what? Get off the track when the account is big enough. Because that's what we're told to do; that's what it's all about."

"That's just it—that's exactly right," Hal said. "I started saving for retirement in my twenties, and I always had a clear plan. Once that retirement account hit a certain size, and then I would know I had enough, and then I'd retire. And that's what I did. The only question I ever asked myself was, 'Do I have enough to retire?' When the answer was yes, I did it. Almost like a reflex. Like autopilot."

"That's my plan," Richard agreed. "I've calculated it'll take me another twelve or fifteen years to get my account to a certain size. And then I'll retire. Because that's what you do."

Hal found himself drumming his fingers on the table, just as he had against the side of his fishing boat. Something was starting to stir inside him.

"All right," he said. "Say I had asked myself more than just that one question before I jumped ship. What if I had taken other factors into consideration? What would they be?" He spread open the paper napkin from the side of his placemat. "You got a pen by any chance?"

"I do," Richard said, pulling a ballpoint out of the pocket of his windbreaker. "I don't know why, but I even carry one around out here in the mountains. Force of habit, I guess."

Hal chuckled. "Boy, do I know the feeling," he said. He took the pen and clicked it, then began to write across the top of the napkin.

Hal drew a rectangle on the left side of the napkin and labeled it "Career." Then he drew an arrow pointing to a circle on the right side of the napkin, which he labeled "Retirement."

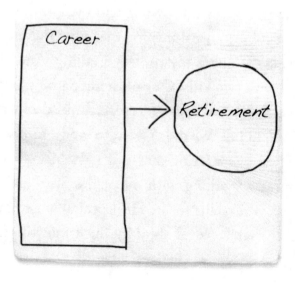

"Okay," he said to Richard. "Maybe you can help me think through this. You're standing in my shoes ten or fifteen years ago, with a successful career, heading toward retirement. So what are all the things you'd put over here in the 'Career' box? What are all the things you're working for right now?"

"Okay, well, let's see," Richard said, gamely jumping in. Like Hal, he wasn't particularly given to launching into conversation with strangers, but he liked Hal and thought he'd brought up some interesting questions. And there was nowhere else to be and nothing pressing to get done out here in the mountains, so he figured he might as well.

"I founded a consultancy firm about ten years ago," Richard started. "That's what takes up most of my time and energy. I'm the sole owner, and I've got three junior-level consultants working for me, plus five people on support staff. That's my professional life. And then I'm married with two kids. One of them, Sam, is just finishing up college, and my wife, Alice, and I decided to pay his tuition in full. We didn't want to saddle him with debt right when he's starting out in life. He's been spending his summers working with me at the firm, and I think he's got a real talent for it. He'll probably get an MBA, and after that we're all thinking he'll join the firm full time. My other son, Peter, is . . . " Richard paused for a moment. "Well, he's had some struggles in life. Alice and I are pretty worried about his future. He's not sure what he wants from life or how to make it happen for himself."

Hal nodded sympathetically. He was jotting down notes quickly as Richard spoke.

"We've got a nice house that's paid for," Richard continued, shifting to other topics. "And a vacation home with a small mortgage. Almost paid for. We lease a couple cars. I go golfing every few weeks with business associates, and I like to take solo hiking trips. And Alice and I travel once a year or so, usually a big trip of about a week or two."

As Richard finished, Hal caught up with him. The rectangle on the left side now looked like this:

"Okay," Hal said, tapping the tip of the pen on the napkin. "This is everything you'll be retiring *from* in fifteen years or so. Now . . . what will you be retiring *to*?"

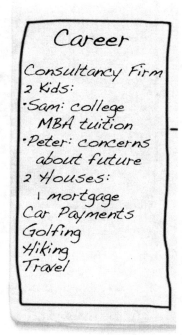

Career

Consultancy Firm
2 Kids:
• Sam: college
   MBA tuition
• Peter: concerns
   about future
2 Houses:
   1 mortgage
Car Payments
Golfing
Hiking
Travel

There was a silence. Finally, Richard said, "More hiking trips in the mountains."

Hal burst into laughter. "That's it!" he exclaimed. "That's just the problem!" He quickly jotted something down and then turned the napkin so that Richard could see it.

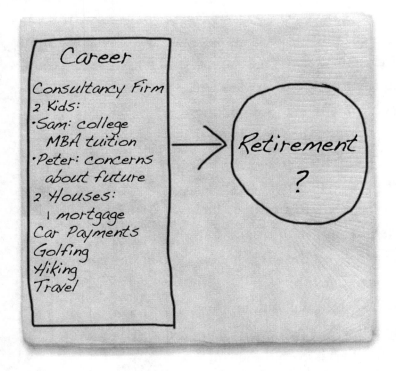

"This is our problem," Hal said. "We've followed life's rules. We toe the line; we're good savers; we take care of our families. And now here I am at what's supposed to be the apex of all of that, and I'm asking, 'Isn't there anything more than this?' And I think it's because I didn't ask myself, 'What am I retiring *to*?' I knew what I was retiring *from*—everybody knows that; that's what we work all our lives to build up. But now I've got this big empty circle—and you're headed for the same thing. What's going to fill it?"

Richard nodded. "I get it. You did the American dream; you worked your tail off all your life, and now it's time to put your feet up and relax. But that's not quite you. Obviously, you deserve a break, but you also still need a reason to get up in the morning. That's only human."

"Right," Hal agreed. "So, what are the questions I should have been asking myself before I retired? How should I have planned what I was going to retire *to*?" He got a fresh napkin from the waitress, and began to jot down notes. "I know the one and only question I *did* ask myself," he said, writing it down.

· *Do I have enough saved to retire?*

"Fair question," Richard said, looking down at the napkin. "So what else would you have asked yourself?"

Hal began to fire off questions, jotting them down as he went.

- *What will I do after I've read the paper each morning?*

- *What's on my bucket list?*

- *How much traveling do Margaret and I want to do?*

- *What charitable organizations could use my skills as a volunteer?*

- *How often would I volunteer?*

- *What do I need in order to feel fulfilled?*

Hal looked up from his list. "Do you know what's occurring to me?" he asked.

Richard shook his head.

"Before I retired, I was asking myself about one number, 'How much do I need to retire?' But the real question should have been about *many* numbers. 'How much money do I need to do each of these things in my retirement?' I need to figure out not only how I want to spend my retirement, but also how I'm going to fund the goals I've set."

Richard nodded his agreement.

"What I need," Hal said almost absentmindedly, "is my own personal manager."

Suddenly, Richard's face lit up. "Hey, that's not a bad idea," he said. "I mean, Alice and I have an advisor who handles our retirement account, but what you're talking about is somebody to help you create a real plan. And somebody to make sure you stick to it."

"Yeah," Hal agreed. "I didn't realize that's what I was talking about, but now it's starting to come together."

"I think I may know someone," Richard said. "A friend of mine named Keith is a Certified Wealth Strategist®, and he's been telling me I should come in for a consultation. I kept saying, 'Thanks, but I don't need to.' I know money; it's a huge part of my job. And Alice and I are doing fine with the advisor we've got—we check in once a year to make sure our investment account keeps growing, and that's it. But this conversation has got me thinking maybe I need to be more proactive. I think I need to find someone who can help me really outline a clear plan—who can look at my financial life from a fresh perspective. Maybe I should make an appointment."

Hal picked up the pen again, jotted down his e-mail address on a corner of the placemat, tore it off, and passed it to Richard. "Would you get in touch with me when you're back in the city?" he asked. "I'd like to meet Keith."

CHAPTER TWO

A Different Kind of Conversation

BACK IN THE city, Richard and Hal sat across from Keith in comfortable leather chairs in a brightly lit office. "If we sit down together in these same chairs three years from today and we look back over the past three years, what would have needed to take place in your life both personally and professionally for you to be happy and successful?" the advisor asked. There was a brief silence. Keith had just posed the essential question—the very question that both Richard and Hal had been trying to articulate since their first meeting at the mountain lodge.

After their shared coffee and brainstorming session, Richard and Hal had agreed to stay in touch after they got back to the city. Both of them had gotten enthused about the retirement questions they'd come up with together, and they'd agreed to do some joint research to see if they could start generating answers. Their first step was to set up a fact-finding meeting with Richard's friend Keith.

Richard's goal, of course, was to put together a clearer plan, from a financial *and* emotional perspective, for his path toward retirement. He wanted something more solid than just continuing to dutifully pay into a 401(k).

Hal's goal was even more urgent: he wanted to start feeling more fulfilled and purposeful in his retirement. He knew, of course, that this would require financial planning, and he was curious to see if Keith had any answers to the questions he'd only thought to ask *after* he ended his career.

Keith was a tall man in his late forties with dark brown hair and a warm smile. Hal had liked him immediately. He had been expecting the same kinds of questions that he'd already gone over a hundred times with his financial advisor: What do you have saved now, and how much risk are you willing to tolerate in your investment strategy? Instead, Keith was taking a very different approach.

"Let me give you some examples," Keith said. "When I ask my clients what needs to come together in their lives over the course of the next three years for them to feel successful, the answer is very rarely how much money they want to have set aside. Instead, they talk to me about *experiences* and *relationships*. They talk to me about what they want their lives to *feel* like.

"People tell me things like:

- **I want to be healthy.**

- **I want to finally take that European vacation I've always thought about.**

- **I want my son or daughter's college tuition to be paid in full.**

- **I want to take my family to Disney World.**

- **I want to be out of debt.**

"And then of course, there's the big one:

- **I want to be retired."**

Richard and Hal sat, mulling this over. "I see what you mean," Richard told Keith. "We tend to think the most important thing is to put our goals in financial terms, but before you can start getting firm about numbers and figures, you have to know what you want to accomplish with that money.

"That's exactly what Hal and I realized we had in common," Richard continued. "We want to have a plan for fulfilling life in retirement, and that's why I finally decided to take you up on your invitation for a consultation. We suddenly realized we needed something a little more thoughtful than your run-of-the-mill financial planning."

Keith smiled. "I'm really glad the two of you came in for this meeting, because if you've already started thinking about these questions beforehand, it means you're well ahead of the game. Oftentimes, people are kind of surprised when I start this conversation. I'm opening up a lot of emotional issues for them that they haven't necessarily considered before—and a lot of them are surprised to be talking about these issues in a financial advisor's office. They're surprised that I'm willing to acknowledge that it's not just a question of what they want to accomplish financially, but also what they want to avoid."

"How so?" Hal asked.

"Well, for example, people tell me that they're worried their children aren't going to be able to manage money if they pass away. Or they're worried the market will go down and they won't be getting enough return on their investments to maintain their lifestyle—or even to get proper care if something should happen to them. Many say to me, 'Keith, *I don't need to be rich, but don't let me be broke.*' People want to know how they can avoid outliving their money."

Hal nodded in agreement. "I see. Of course, all of these questions have always been in the back of my mind, but my advisor never put it out in the open like this. We didn't talk in terms of what my life looks like and what my goals and concerns are, the main question was, 'Am I hitting certain benchmarks in my portfolio?'"

"Unfortunately, that's pretty standard practice," Keith said. "There are too many advisors out there who have preconceived plans that they want to fit their clients into. They start with the plan and mold the clients to fit it, rather than starting with the clients' circumstances and molding a plan around them.

"Many advisors look at the age group you're in, your demographics, etc., and then try to pigeonhole you into a certain type of investment strategy or asset class. But the advising relationship isn't about me and the clever tricks I've worked out ahead of time. It's about finding out what is important to you and then funding it. That's why it is so crucial that I get aligned with what clients envision for themselves."

"And what if people aren't quite sure what they envision for themselves?" Richard asked, almost tentatively.

"That's exactly the point of the discussion," Keith said, sitting back in his chair with an easy smile. "You don't have to know right away; the point is to get the wheels turning and to start thinking about these questions before they jump up and bite you.

"I actually had a great example come up just today of what can happen when the big questions sneak up on you," Keith continued. "A couple came in for their first consultation this morning. They're in their late sixties, and the husband was the primary breadwinner. The wife worked part-time throughout her life, but her main focus was raising their three children. So, the husband just retired a couple months ago, and the two of them are suddenly together around the house more than they've ever been in their forty-year marriage.

"And do you know what the wife said to me?" Keith asked. "She said, 'We can't get out of each other's hair!' The emotional transition took them by surprise. So of course we had financial questions to work out together, but the main purpose of our conversation this morning was to come up with a list of activities, from traveling to volunteerism, that would make the two of them feel fulfilled now that they're in this stage of life. From there, we'll figure out the finances to support those activities."

Hal shifted in his seat. "I'm half surprised and half relieved to hear you tell that story, Keith," he said. "Because my wife, Margaret, said the exact same thing to me a couple of weeks ago: 'You're always in my hair.' One of the main reasons I got so engaged in this project with Richard is that I know things can't be right in my relationship when I'm feeling at a loss for what to do in my retirement.

"Margaret and I never had problems before," Hal continued. "We were high school sweethearts, and we've raised two really great kids. But then it hit me for the first time: our relationship has always been structured around my work.

"I had to put a lot into securing and fulfilling speaking engagements. I had to be my own boss and manage my income so that I could support a family as a self-employed entrepreneur. And I was traveling about two weeks out of every month. It never occurred to me until I retired how much that defined our home life and how much support Margaret provided throughout all of it. To be perfectly honest, these six months since I've been retired have been the most stressful in our marriage."

"You're absolutely not alone in feeling that way," Keith said. "I've had many other clients tell me that the early part of retirement involved reimagining their marriages. What I can help you with in that area is setting clear goals so that you feel as motivated in this stage of your life as you did during your career.

"I'll tell you candidly," Keith went on, "that many of the people I meet who don't ask themselves, 'What is my retirement really about? What is going to put a smile on my face?' end up with physical ailments, and unfortunately, some even die young. But those who really find a reason to get moving live well into their eighties and beyond. It gratifies me to be a part of that broader conversation. Not just, 'How much do I need and when?' but 'Why? What do I want to use this money for? What value is it going to bring to my life?'"

"I'm curious to know," Hal said, "how you started working these questions into your practice. I've never had another advisor take quite this approach."

"Great question!" Keith said. "It's something that has developed over years of working with people and noticing that we just don't have a solid springboard to work from if we don't have the initial discussion about the questions that people avoid or don't think to ask.

"It really started to come together for me more than a decade ago, when my wife and I were planning for our daughter's college education. Our daughter was only ten at the time, and my wife and I were reviewing the college savings fund we had opened for her when she was born. Suddenly, the question came up: What about her wedding? So we decided to open an account for that, too.

"That really started the wheels turning for me. Why do we keep just one savings account that we pile all the money into, when we're saving for all kinds of different things? How can we really budget for each individual item, track our progress toward each goal, and stay motivated if we're just looking at this one, abstract number?

"People give to church every week because it's what you're supposed to do, but they don't start to write the big checks until the church says, 'We need a new roof, and we're having a drive to raise the funds for it.' That's when people come out of the woodwork. It's hard to set money aside when it's for some abstract reason, but when you have clear, budgeted goals, everything changes.

"So," Keith continued, "my wife and I opened five new investment accounts and named them. Five separate 'buckets,' if you will, that we put money into each month. A college fund, a wedding fund, a second home fund, a travel fund, and an opportunity fund—in case something unexpected and exciting comes up for us that we want to be able to take advantage of.

"And now I talk to my clients in terms of those buckets. I've found that it meets two needs for us: first, it solves the problem of getting people to budget—because that's what most people are missing. They want to know when they can retire, but they don't know whether they need three thousand dollars a month in order to live . . . or seven thousand.

"And the second problem it solves is that it gets people excited about all this. This is the area that people can really enjoy. Instead of thinking, *I just have to keep putting my nose to the grindstone until I have this large, daunting sum of money in my 401(k)*, they can start thinking in terms of, *I'm saving this amount for the European vacation and this amount for my children's future*. It starts to inject a little meaning into the numbers."

Both Richard and Hal were smiling broadly.

"You're absolutely right," Richard agreed. "This does add a little enjoyment to the process. And it appeals to my way of thinking as a consultant. It's strategic and goal-oriented."

Hal nodded enthusiastically. "I'd really like to start talking this over with Margaret. I'm starting to feel a lot better about this phase of my life already, and I think she'd agree."

"Well, from here," Keith said, "I'd love to bring both of your wives into the planning if you think you'd like to continue the conversation with me. This really is about life planning, so I think it's important to involve the whole family."

"Absolutely," Richard said, "I'd love to get Alice involved, too. It's almost like you've gotten me thinking about planning for the next phase of my life. Not retirement, but just a new phase in which I might work far less and have more time to travel, more time with my kids and maybe someday my grandkids. I've got a lot to ask Alice about—like what kinds of buckets she'd like us to create."

"I can help get that conversation started," Keith said, passing them each a folder of materials. "This is my planning guide—it's a tool I offer clients to help you start budgeting and deciding what kinds of buckets you'd like to set up for different goals."

As he said this, Keith stood up, offering Richard and Hal warm handshakes. "And my suggestion for you when you start this conversation with your wives," he said as he walked them to the door, "is to begin with the same question we started with . . . "

• • •

Over the next three years, what needs to take place in your life, personally and professionally, for you to feel happy and successful?*

CHAPTER THREE

A Comprehensive Planning Guide

"I HAVE TO say, I'm really relieved you're bringing this up," Alice said to Richard. The two of them were sitting together in their sunlit kitchen, where they had just finished breakfast. They had agreed to set aside the morning to look at the materials Keith had given Richard—which included links to some web site—and to start thinking about the questions his planning guide raised.

They were sitting at their small, blond wood kitchen table. They had cleared the breakfast dishes together and spread out the planning guide on the table between them.

"When you first said you wanted to meet with Keith," Alice said, "I didn't understand why. I figured since we have a financial advisor and you said our retirement account is in order, why rock the boat? But I'm starting to see that what Keith offers is much more than just monitoring our investments. He's really going to help us start answering all those little nagging questions that we keep putting off for later."

"That's exactly it," Richard agreed. "It seems like for the longest time I've been avoiding getting clarity on a retirement plan because it seems so far in the future, but now that I actually have some guidance on what questions to ask and what information we need to gather, it feels like a weight has lifted."

The planning guide that Keith had given them was essentially a scorecard that allowed them to gather all their personal data into one place. It was exactly what Keith promised it would be—a springboard to help them start answering the questions that Hal and Richard had first raised when they met at the mountain lodge.

Together, Richard and Alice carefully went over each page of the planning guide. The guide broke down complex questions into smaller ones so that they could come up with answers step by step. Keith had told them not to worry too much about filling in details yet—his staff would help them by working from financial documents they would provide, such as their bank and investment statements and their tax returns from prior years.

When it was completed, the planning guide would give them a complete record of their financial situation: What was their net worth as a couple? Who owned which of their assets? Who were the beneficiaries of their assets? What kind of insurance policies did they have? All of these questions (and many more) would be answered.

The most interesting part of the document to Richard was the budgeting portion. Once upon a time, he and Alice had estimated the monthly income they'd like to have in their retirement so that they could tell their current financial advisor what they wanted to retire on. But when they came up with that figure they hadn't factored in their "bucket list"—their hopes and dreams and the things they wanted to accomplish. The planning guide that Keith had given them was helping them to get that conversation started.

As he and Alice came to the portion of the planning guide that discussed buckets, Richard said, "While Hal and I were talking, it occurred to me for the first time that I need to think ahead about all the things I want to do to continue to feel fulfilled in life once I'm no longer CEO of the firm. It's a pretty big question. *Who will I be when I'm not a consultant and entrepreneur anymore?* The thing that comes to mind first is that I want to have a 'hiking bucket,' so maybe I can take some of the longer trips that I've always dreamed about."

"What about hiking a part of the Pacific Crest Trail?" Alice suggested, brightening.

"You read my mind!" Richard said. He had occasionally mentioned the trail to Alice as a sort of "maybe someday" idea, but he hadn't realized that she had actually taken his dream to heart.

"You might even be able to bring one of the boys with you, depending on what's going on in their lives," Alice said.

"You know, that's not a bad idea," Richard agreed. "It couldn't hurt for Peter and I to spend more time together and really connect over something. I know sometimes he feels like Sam and I are two peas in a pod and he's the odd one out."

"I think it would be a great idea for you and Peter to hike the trail together," Alice said. "I do worry about how he will feel when Sam moves into your role at the firm. I wish we could help him find more of a sense of purpose in life."

What both Richard and Alice were skirting around but having trouble saying out loud was that they were genuinely fearful for their son Peter. He was still very young—only twenty—and had struggled with a drug addiction in the year after he had graduated from high school. With his parents' love and support, he had gone to rehab and was now doing relatively well. He had a job at a record store and his own apartment not far from Richard and Alice's home.

But the possibility that Peter could relapse was a cloud of worry that followed Richard and Alice. A particular difficulty for them was that their first son, Sam, had such a glowing record by comparison: he was a straight-A student who was very much his father's son, and he was already an outstanding summer associate in Richard's firm. It was almost a given that he would follow in his father's footsteps as CEO. As proud as they were of Sam, both Richard and Alice worried about how to treat their sons equally and make sure that they both felt like loved and essential members of the family.

"I'm starting to think that maybe the kind of planning we're doing right now is a good place for us to start helping Peter however we can," Richard said. "Of course, he's got to find his own way, but maybe Keith can help us come up with a plan so that he and Sam are both taken care of fairly if something happens to us . . .

even if they are two very different young men with very different paths."

Alice nodded thoughtfully. "Let's set that aside as something we want to discuss with Keith in greater depth," she suggested. Richard agreed.

The two of them turned back to the list of buckets they were making. It now read:

- Hiking

- European travel

- Eliminate vacation home mortgage

- Charitable giving

- Provide for Sam and Peter

"I never would have thought that this could be fun," Alice said, "but looking at this list, I'm starting to feel pretty excited about planning for our future!"

"Me too," Richard said, smiling at Alice. "And even the less fun questions in this planning guide . . . they aren't exactly a barrel of laughs to think about, but

I actually feel relieved that we're talking about them ahead of time.

"Some of these I never would have thought to consider," Richard continued, paging through the planning guide. "Like this one, about long-term care insurance. It's good to have a little nudge in the right direction."

Alice nodded soberly. She had been quietly bringing up the subject of a will and a power of attorney with Richard for a few years, and she was frankly glad to see that the planning guide mentioned these important documents as well. She tapped the page lightly with the end of her pencil. "And here's where we'll eventually put information about our will," she said. "Looks like Keith is on my side on this question—it's important to have it in order."

Richard nodded ruefully. "I guess what this planning guide is really doing for us is helping me see the holes in my planning," he said.

"That's another topic we'll set aside to discuss more when we see Keith," Alice said with an affectionate smile. "Hey, look at this," she said, turning the page. "It says, '13 Wealth Management Issues.'"

Richard looked down at the page and read through the checklist, item by item.

1. Investments

2. Insurance

3. Liabilities

4. Qualified Retirement Plan/IRA

5. Stock Options

6. Business Succession Plan

7. Durable Power of Attorney

8. Gifting to Children/Descendants

9. Charitable Gifting During Life

10. Titling of Assets

11. Executor/Trustee

12. Distribution Plan at Death to Spouse/
    Descendants

13. Charitable Inclinations at Death

"Wow," Alice said. "This is a great checklist. Not everything applies to us, but this pretty much covers all the big issues that could come up for us in terms of planning for our financial future."

"I'm sure Keith will help us tick through each of these items one by one," Richard said. "It's really helpful to have it all in one place like this, though."

Alice leaned over and gave Richard a kiss on the cheek. "I'm really glad you decided to meet with Keith," she said again. "I'm looking forward to doing this planning together."

CHAPTER FOUR

Bringing the Whole Family On Board

KEITH GAVE BOTH Richard and Alice a warm handshake when they arrived in his office two weeks later.

"Alice," Keith said, "I'm so glad you were able to come in with Richard. He and I didn't want to get any deeper into the conversation without including you."

"I'm glad, too," Alice agreed. "I have to be honest—I was a bit skeptical at first, because Richard and I already have an investment advisor. But now I'm starting to see that what you're offering us goes way beyond managing our account. And to be honest, it's nice to feel like I have an ally in getting Richard to plan ahead. He's got a lot on his plate at the firm, so sometimes it's tough to get him to set time aside for this kind of thing."

Richard laughed good-naturedly. "Are you telling on me?" he asked Alice playfully. Then he turned to Keith.

"She's absolutely right, though. At work I'm dealing with corporations that have multimillion-dollar revenue streams, and we're always looking ahead five, ten, and twenty years down the road. I don't know why it never occurred to me to apply that same kind of strategizing to my own home life. I guess I fell into the trap of thinking that if I had a 401(k), I was doing everything that needed doing.

"It was really Hal who opened my eyes to the bigger picture," Richard continued, "and to the fact that I need to plan for the future in a more holistic way that includes not just my finances but also my personal goals and my relationships with my family . . . and my sons in particular."

Keith nodded. "That's really what all this is about. It's easy to get caught up in the numbers and figures and to forget what those things represent—the experiences and the relationships in life. That's what I'm most interested in. That's why I do what I do. The reality is that there are any number of advisors out there who have the skill and the knowledge to find decent investments for you. What makes what I do different from the typical advising relationship is that I'm ready to roll up my sleeves and help you ask the tough questions. My goal is to help you make a plan that takes into account where you want to be and where you are right now so that we can think realistically about how to get from A to B."

Alice smiled. "That *is* different from the conversations we have with our current advisor," she agreed.

Keith's unique approach to the advising relationship had developed over time, through trial and error, and by getting to know his clients on a human level. But he had actually known at a fairly young age that he was passionate about helping people take stock of their financial lives and about helping people to set goals.

When Keith was fourteen years old, he'd wanted to start saving money to buy a car, and so his parents had told him that he could work toward his goal. He'd taken a job working for his uncle, who owned a fish market where he sold fresh fish from the surrounding lakes. When Keith first approached his uncle about a job, his uncle had said, "Great! I'll pay you $500 a month." To Keith, earning $1,500 in one summer sounded great—so he agreed.

He soon learned that what had sounded like a lot of money to his fourteen-year-old mind wasn't actually all that much when it was stacked up against working from 7:00 a.m. to 6:00 p.m. five days a week all summer. He also realized that the money was harder to hang onto than he'd expected—especially when there were other things he wanted to do and to buy besides that car looming in the distant future.

That summer was when Keith began to really understand the value of a dollar and the value of careful planning and staying accountable to the goals you set for yourself. The experience was just a small seed for what would become his life's work.

"I want to start today's conversation," Keith said to Richard and Alice, "by getting a really clear picture of how you envision your future as a family. That will help me formulate a financial plan for how you're going to get there. The planning guide I gave you is a great tool because it helps us identify the gaps in your planning that we should fill in together so that you have a comprehensive, rather than a piecemeal, approach to preparing for the future.

"But before we get there, let's start at the beginning. Have the two of you given any more thought to where you want to be three years from today, personally and professionally?"

Alice nodded. "We talked a lot about that question," she said. "And I think the answer is that both of us still see retirement as being quite a ways down the road."

Although Richard was the primary breadwinner in the family, Alice had worked for most of their marriage, taking only a few years away from her job as an elementary school teacher when their sons were very little. She loved her work, and her teaching schedule still allowed her plenty of time with the boys, especially when they were all on summer vacation together.

"Retirement is probably twelve or fifteen years away," Alice continued, "but over the next three years, I think we'd like to start laying the foundation for slowing down our careers. To us, that means paying off our vacation home mortgage so that we can turn our attention to retirement savings. I think we'd like to feel confident that we're on the way to retiring comfortably. And that includes thinking about options for providing for our sons."

"That makes perfect sense," Keith said, "and it's right in line with what most folks your age are concerned with. Even though retirement is still a ways off for you, now is a great time to start planning so that you have some of the mechanisms in place that take some time to yield results. So why don't we take a look at retirement income first? Then we'll move on to the finer details of your financial future, such as insurance and planning for your sons."

Keith got out a remote control and turned on a screen hanging on the wall above his desk. "When Richard was last here," he explained, "I gave him a checklist of all the documents that I'd need to look at to help me come up with a comprehensive plan for the two of you."

Richard had dropped off those documents—which included tax returns from the two prior years, bank and investment statements, Social Security statements, and some of the family's insurance policies and legal documents—about a week earlier.

"I've had some time to go through those documents," Keith continued, "and I've come up with some projections. You mentioned to me that you'd like to get your vacation home mortgage paid off in the next three years, so let's take that into account when we look at these projections. That means that for the next three years, you may be saving slightly less as you funnel more money into your mortgage payments—but three years out, you should see a pretty big jump in the value of your accounts as you're able to start setting more aside."

Using graphs on the screen, Keith walked them through some hypothetical investment reports that showed them the potential value of their investments—their 401(k) and their separate IRAs—in one figure. He showed them projections for the next ten, twenty, and thirty years, working under the assumption that they would retire within fifteen years.[1]

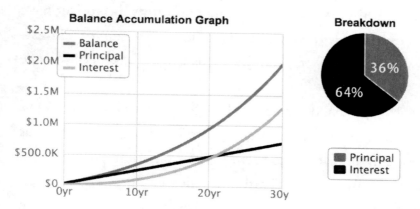

"Something I noticed as I was preparing this presentation for you," Keith said, "is that a phenomenon has happened in your accounts that I see often. In the industry, we call it 'overlap,' and it basically means that you have these investment accounts without necessarily diversifying the investments in them. It can happen pretty easily."

Keith continued with an explanation. "Just as an example," he said, "if you have five separate accounts, those separate accounts might contain investments in the same companies. You're collecting the same investments rather than truly diversifying, which is of course what

1 Source: http://www.calculator.net/investment-calculator.html

we recommend to make sure you're minimizing risk and continuing to make as much progress as possible."

Here, Keith brought up a table that showed Richard and Alice where a few of their accounts did in fact have overlap. He then walked them through a plan for reinvesting and showed them how this might make a difference over time.

Keith had separated their investments into 'buckets' that reflected what Richard and Alice had highlighted as being important to them in their planning guide. Using these buckets, Richard and Alice could see how much they would need to continue setting aside for goals like traveling to Europe and helping their son Sam with his tuition.

After they had gone over everything, Richard and Alice had a clearer picture of what their retirement income from investments might look like if they each chose to retire at sixty, sixty-two, or sixty-four. They also had a rough sense of how much they could spend on a trip to Europe and when, how much they could contribute to Sam's tuition if he decided to get an MBA, and roughly what they could afford to spend on buckets such as charitable giving and Richard's solo hiking trips.

"Now, here's the other question mark I think the two of you should consider," Keith continued. "Social Security income. Most financial advisors are going to tell you to start collecting on Social Security as soon as you are legally able. They usually advise you to do this for two reasons: 1) They haven't thoroughly studied the power of compounding Social Security benefits, and 2) it is easy to turn on your Social Security income since it's available, and this allows you to take less money out of your investment accounts. They're taking the path of least resistance rather than taking the time to look at each and every angle." Richard and Alice both listened intently—they were impressed that Keith was willing to be so upfront with them.

"But it's actually a better deal for you—if you can afford it and are healthy—to delay your Social Security benefits. I'll show you why." He pulled up a bar graph on his screen that showed various Social Security incomes at various ages.[2]

"If you retire at 66, you start receiving 100 percent of your monthly benefits at that time. Just as an example,

---

2 Source: http://www.fool.com/retirement/general/2014/09/21/why-smart-people-take-social-security-benefits-ear.aspx

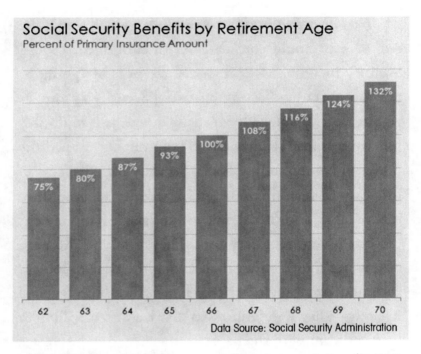

Social Security Benefits by Retirement Age
Percent of Primary Insurance Amount

75% · 80% · 87% · 93% · 100% · 108% · 116% · 124% · 132%

62 63 64 65 66 67 68 69 70

Data Source: Social Security Administration

let's say Richard could potentially start receiving $2,000 per month at age 66. Now, if he 'turns on' that income at 66, he'll continue to receive that $2,000 a month for the rest of his life. Alice, you could begin to receive the same as a survivor benefit if you outlive him. But that income isn't going to increase, except for a small allowance for inflation.

"Now, if Richard decides to wait to 'turn on' those benefits, the monthly benefit goes up each year by 8 percent from age 66 to age 70. So, if Richard waits until age

67 to start collecting Social Security, he gets 108 percent of his benefits monthly for the rest of his life. At 68, he gets 116 percent. And so on.

"So, taking my previous example, if he starts collecting at 66, he gets $2,000 a month. But if he starts collecting at 67, he gets $2,160 a month . . . and if he waits all the way until age 70, he could collect $2,640 a month for the rest of his life. And don't forget that if Richard passes away, Alice will get the equivalent of that dollar amount.

"Now, I can't guarantee you an 8 percent return on your investments in the marketplace. So in that sense, Social Security is actually a more powerful way to grow your income. My advice, then, is usually to keep some cash out of the market that you live on until your Social Security is more valuable."

"Wow," Richard said, "I can't believe this is the first time I'm hearing about this."

"It comes as a surprise to most people," Keith said. "So in anticipation of that, I went ahead and ran a Social Security analysis for the two of you." He pulled the analysis up on the screen, showing them each their projected Social Security income at ages 62 (if they decided to start collecting early—in which case they'd receive less than 100 percent of their benefits), 66, and 70.

"Now these figures may change over the next ten years, if you have significant changes in your income," Keith explained. "So you don't have to make a decision now about when you want to 'turn on' those benefits. But I would strongly recommend that we get together and have another conversation before you do start collecting, so that you have a clear sense of the pros and cons. We'll set it on the backburner until the time comes."

"Great," Richard said, exchanging a smile with Alice. This meeting with Keith was already proving to be incredibly valuable, and they were only just getting started.

CHAPTER FIVE

Where Are Your Gaps?

AS THEIR MEETING continued, Keith, Richard, and Alice turned their attention from the big picture of retirement planning to a more detail-oriented perspective.

"So far we've been talking about your future from a bird's-eye view," Keith said. "But now I'd like to zoom in and look at some of the gaps in your planning guide. Have you given any thought to how you want to handle your long-term care expenses?"

There was a brief silence, and finally Alice said, "Well, it's one of the areas that we noticed as we were filling out the planning guide that we don't really have a clear plan for. It comes up every now and then, but we keep kicking the can down the road."

"I absolutely understand," Keith said, "and you're not alone. But I'm glad I've got you in the office now, because you're actually at a good age to think about purchasing a policy. If you delay it much longer, you won't get as much bang for your buck, but right now you can get pretty good coverage."

Alice nodded. "Then I'm glad you're giving us the little push we need," she said, exchanging a meaningful glance with Richard.

"I consider helping you plan for long-term care to be part of my job," Keith said, "because if you don't have coverage, long-term care is going to swallow up your savings—and all the work we've done together—pretty quickly. So I work with professionals who help me offer appropriate plan options and quotes to my clients. Through my relationships with these insurance specialists, I can help you get a policy solidified.

"There are a couple of ways to purchase insurance: most commonly, you either use it or you lose it. For a lot of policies, if you never go to a long-term care facility, the money that you pay into the policy is gone. But there are some policies that will allow your survivors to get some of the money back as a death benefit if it isn't paid out toward long-term care."

Keith gave the two of them some handouts and explained what kind of information he would need from them to help them apply for a policy. He explained that after they had chosen and secured a policy, he would factor it into their expenses and adjust their financial plan accordingly.

"So, as you can see," Keith continued, "we're moving into end-of-life territory and looking ahead for how you want to take care of your loved ones should something happen to you. It's perfectly natural to not have all of these ducks in a row—it's no one's favorite topic. But I've found with a lot of my clients that they actually start to feel pretty good once these things are taken care of, because they have some peace of mind knowing that their spouse or children won't have to sort through this stuff—or worse yet, be denied access to the assets or money that should go to them.

"Now, in this regard, I think of myself as one member of a team of professionals who are all going to work together to get things in order for you—and that team includes your CPA, your attorney, and your banking professionals. The thing is, these professionals usually only consider their own piece of the puzzle, but I'm interested in looking at the whole puzzle once it's put together, because it's my job to help you plan for your *whole* future. So while we might bring in an attorney to help you complete a trust, for example, I'll work with you to figure out how that trust fits into the larger picture."

Keith paused—Alice and Richard were starting to look a bit overwhelmed. "The good news is that there's no rush to get all of this done today," he said. "You've done yourselves a favor by getting the ball rolling relatively early, so we can take some time to look at these things step by step until we feel like the whole planning guide is filled in and you're covered in terms of a will, power of attorney, health care directives, and possibly trusts for your sons.

"Looking into these 'gaps' ensures that things you thought were taken care of don't fall through the cracks. Here's an example that comes up often: you can fill out a very simple form, called a 'paid on death,' at the bank to specify a beneficiary to your checking or savings account. Most people don't realize that they need to take this step in order for their next of kin to receive that money should they pass away. If there's no beneficiary specified, the funds in your account will become what are called 'probated assets,' and your kids will need to go through a legal procedure to get the money. But if you fill out this simple form, your sons can receive the money through an immediate transfer simply by giving the bank a copy of the death certificate.

"Or here's another example," Keith continued. "I had a client whose son was thirty-two years old when he developed a life-threatening infection and ended up in the hospital. He almost died. Thank God he pulled through, but while he was in the hospital, his responsibilities fell to his dad because he was single. He had a house payment to make, but his dad wasn't legally able to find out how much the payment was. So the father started blindly putting $2,000 a month into his son's bank account, hoping it would cover the automatic mortgage payments. With a power of attorney, you can avoid that sort of bureaucratic hang-up. You can clear people to have access to information or to make decisions for you.

"That's the kind of thing I can help you organize," Keith said. "The other professionals in your life may not be looking at things quite so holistically, so they may not see these gaps in paperwork and preparation. Over time, we'll go through the whole planning guide step by step and get all of these documents in one place so that you have peace of mind, knowing everything that could come up is accounted for."

"This is all really wonderful," Alice said. "And I agree that it's best if we take some time to go through it, since it's clear that Richard and I do have gaps in our planning."

She hesitated for a moment, taking Richard's hand before shifting to a subject that was difficult for both of them. "But there's one more thing that I would feel better if we talked about today. And that's our sons and planning for their future."

Richard nodded gravely. "You know a little bit about the struggle Alice and I have had with our younger son, Peter. He's doing a lot better now; he's working, and he's been sober for a year. But we have serious concerns about his ability to manage money. And as my firm does better and better, and our older son, Sam, is more and more a part of that success, we're worried that Peter will feel like he's getting left behind. But at the same time, it's just not realistic to include him in the succession plan for my business."

Keith nodded. "I'm glad you brought this up," he said, "because it was the last topic I wanted to make sure we cover today. You're voicing a concern that I have seen arise with other clients. The solution that I offer is that there are ways to treat all adult children *equitably* but not *equally*."

"How do you mean?" Richard asked.

"Well, it sounds like Sam is probably going to finish his undergraduate degree, get his MBA, and move into a leadership role in your company. There's every reason to believe that you'll eventually work with your board of directors to put a succession plan in place so that ownership of the firm transfers to Sam. And your firm is actually quite valuable.

"Now, Peter's interests and aptitudes don't lie with the firm, and it's also a wiser bet not to hand him a lot of financial responsibility at one time, given his history of addiction. But at the same time, you want to be fair to him. If Sam inherits this valuable company, where does that leave Peter?"

"Exactly!" Alice said, her face somewhat drawn with worry. "This is really something that keeps us up at night. Our sons are very different, but they do have a strong relationship, and we want to support that. We don't want to inadvertently create resentment between them. After all, they're still going to be a family after we're gone."

"You're not at all alone in that feeling," Keith said. "I've heard other clients express the same worries—and there is a solution. In fact, I recently worked with a farming family that has a son and two daughters, and I think their story will be similar to yours. The son stands to inherit the farm, which is quite valuable, but the daughters have moved to the city and have careers, so they won't be involved in the farm operations, and it doesn't make sense to make them partial owners.

"What we did to ensure that the daughters will still receive similar assets when their parents pass was to take out a life insurance policy that is actually owned by his two daughters. When he passes, the son will receive the farm, and the daughters will split the value of the life insurance policy between them. Ultimately, everything comes out to about the same value.

"We can apply the same type of solution here. I can help you create a life insurance policy, Richard, that will benefit Peter upon your death. The company itself will go to Sam. Although the payment that Peter receives from the life insurance policy won't be equal to the value of the company, it will be very close in value. So they're being treated equitably, if not equally.

"Then there still remains the question of whether it's wise to saddle Peter with a large sum of money all at once. My suggestion is that this is the kind of situation that lends itself well to creating trusts. With the help of your attorney, we can create a trust for Peter. When you pass, your life insurance payment will be paid directly into the trust. That way, Peter doesn't receive one large check that he has to decide how to manage at the same time that he's just lost a parent.

"You'll appoint a trustee to oversee this money, with the understanding that it is for Peter and his welfare. That trustee can be anyone. A family member—maybe even Sam—or a close friend or a board member of your company. If Peter decides to go to college and he needs tuition money, if he wants to start a business and needs some seed money, or if someday he's doing really well and would just like to receive a monthly income, the trustee can approve those withdrawals at his or her discretion.

"We can do the same with any personal assets you and Alice would like to pass on to Sam and Peter. Any cash left in your accounts or the value of your investments can either be distributed to them immediately upon your death, or it can be funneled into the trust.

"Again, it's all about coming up with a plan that's equitable, even though it's not equal. We can work it out so that Sam and Peter both get the same amount of net worth, but they might not get it at the same time and in the same form. How does that sound to you?"

Both Richard and Alice had visibly relaxed. "'Equitably

but not equally,'" Richard repeated. "I like the sound of that."

"Me too," Alice agreed. "It would be a real weight off our shoulders to know that we've provided for Peter in a way that will help him be successful."

"That's exactly what a trust can allow for," Keith said. "I can help you work with your attorney to put the documents in place."

"Could we start that process now and then potentially edit the terms of the trust later?" Richard asked. "I don't think my board of directors and I are quite ready yet to put a succession plan for the company in motion. We're pretty confident in Sam's abilities, but retirement is still a ways off for me, and he hasn't finished his education yet. So the exact way we want to split our assets between Sam and Peter may change after it's more clear when and how Sam will take over the business."

"Sure," Keith said. "We can take out the life insurance policy now and create a trust so that you have some peace of mind that it's taken care of should something unexpected happen tomorrow. But we can leave some flexibility so that the terms can be changed as your retirement approaches and as Peter becomes more stable. Ten years from now you may decide, for example, that he needs less oversight from a trustee. With your attorney's help, we can always make those amendments."

"That sounds great," Richard said. He gave Alice's hand a reassuring squeeze. "I have to admit that Alice and I have avoided this conversation. It took all of our focus and energy to help Peter get sober, so we've been sidelining the longer-term questions. But I feel a lot better knowing that we're covering our bases."

Alice nodded her agreement. "If something does happen to us," she said, "that will be enough for the boys to deal with. We wouldn't want to add to their burden by leaving them with legal issues. It's a real comfort to know that there is an answer to this and we can work it out together."

"The last thing I would suggest," Keith said, "is that as we work out these details together, you communicate them clearly to your sons. To go back to the example I gave of my clients who own the farm, they made it very clear to their daughters what the life insurance policy was and how it will work so that they understand that there is a plan in place for them even though their brother is going to inherit the farm. After all, you want everybody to be able to sit down and have happy Thanksgiving dinners together when all is said and done."

Alice smiled. "That's a great idea. Both boys are going to be home for dinner this weekend, and we'll talk to them then."

"Great," Keith said. "You know, we've really covered a lot of territory today. We've looked at:

- **Future retirement income**

- **Asset allocation**

- **Social Security analysis**

- **Options for long-term care planning**

- **Paid on death, power of attorney, and health care directives**

- **Life insurance policies**

- **Trusts**

"At this point," Keith continued, "we've really created a plan for filling in all the gaps in your life planning guide. I'd say that's not too bad for one meeting."

"I agree," said Richard, enthusiastically. "I can't wait to thank Hal for getting me started with all of this."

"Actually," Keith said, "you can say hello to him on your way out. He and his wife, Margaret, are coming in for an appointment right now."

CHAPTER SIX

We Can Do This!
Simple Solutions

"THE TWO OF you have done an excellent job of organizing your financial life," Keith said to Hal and Margaret as they settled in for their consultation. "Looking over your planning guide, you've prepared for Hal's retirement expertly. Your income and your expenses are well matched; you have all of the recommended insurance policies in place; and you've got a will prepared that sets up clear terms for passing on assets to your two children."

Keith paused. "But I think there's still a way of reorganizing your life in retirement that I can offer you that you might not have considered before," he said.

"That's exactly why we're here!" Hal exclaimed.

Margaret smiled. "We are hoping that there's a way of thinking about Hal's retirement that we just don't know about yet. Because you're right: Hal is a great planner, and he's got the family's finances very well taken care of. We don't have any concerns about how our children will be provided for when we pass away or what will happen if we need nursing care or something like that.

"But even though all of that is taken care of," Margaret said, "it just seems like retirement has been a bit of a disappointment for Hal. And if he's at home feeling disappointed and at a loss for what to do, that affects me, too. So what we're really looking for is some thoughts on how to reorganize ourselves so that both of us, together, feel like we have more options for what to do in this new phase of our lives."

"Exactly," Keith agreed. "The first thing I want you to realize is that this is a common phase to go through, and that it's actually a good thing that you're grappling with these questions. Some folks ignore these questions and try to tell themselves that they're satisfied when they really aren't. These people usually run into much more difficult problems. So even though it's not entirely comfortable to feel like you're facing a lot of unknowns, I'm glad you're facing them—that's the only way to resolve them."

Keith got out his remote control and turned on the screen above his desk again. "Where I come into this process is in allocating your resources to help ensure you have the financial freedom to do the things you've always wanted to do in retirement. That's the area that I've noticed is missing in your financial plan."

Keith showed them what he meant with a few charts on the screen. "You have solid investment income, and the two of you have wiggle room to take advantage of and really enjoy the spare time you have now. But right now, things aren't clearly divided up and earmarked—and in my experience, if people don't get specific about how and when they want to use their money, they tend to feel like they can't use it—or, conversely, they spend it all in one place."

"It sounds like you're referring to the 'buckets' we noticed when we were filling out the life planning guide together," Hal said, brightening. "We both really liked the idea of breaking down our savings, and we had fun coming up with our list of buckets."

"Right," Keith agreed. "That's exactly where I'm headed. But before we get there, I want to offer you a suggestion for a different way to split your resources between available cash and investments. It may sound a bit radical to you because many financial advisors don't think in these terms.

"I call it MMR—Managing Money in Retirement," Keith continued. "Some of my clients are high net worth, and they just don't need to worry about outliving their savings. But for most of my clients, outliving savings is a real concern. I mentioned this to you when you were last here with Richard. The theme that I hear is: 'Keith, I don't need to be rich, but don't let me be broke.' Especially after what happened in the economy in 2008, I have a lot of newly retired clients who are very fearful about having to go back to work just to make ends meet. They saw it happen to their colleagues, their friends, their loved ones—and they're scared that it could happen to them."

"Sure," Hal said. "I think that's never far from our minds in today's economy."

"So, here's the work-around that I propose," Keith said. "I'll give you a little background information first. We call the phase of your life when you're in your career the 'accumulation phase.' You're accumulating money to add to your investments. In terms of the returns on those investments, all that matters during the accumulation phase is the average. Even if there are some really bad years like 2007 and 2008, if you average them out across a forty-year career, it's not something to worry about. The bad years could come toward the beginning of your career or toward the end or somewhere in between, and your total at the end would still be the same.

"But when you're in the retirement phase, or the 'distribution phase,' when you stop putting in money and start making withdrawals on your investments, a few down years in the market can really start to matter. Especially in the beginning, a phenomenon that we in the industry call 'sequence of returns' starts to have a large impact.

"Let's say that when you're in the accumulation phase, between age 55 and 65, there are five down years and five up years. It doesn't matter what order those years come in. When you get to age 65, you'll still have the same amount of money. But now imagine that you're in the distribution phase, and there are five down years and five up years. Well, if the five up years come first, you're probably okay. You're making withdrawals on the account, but the account is also growing, so you've got a little cushion for when those down years roll around.

"But say the down years come first. You're making withdrawals on the account, *and* the money invested in the market is dropping. Your account might hit zero before the market has a chance to turn around again. The sequence of returns suddenly matters, because if bad returns come first in the sequence, there might not be enough time to wait for things to average out.

"Imagine you've got a million bucks in the market, and in your distribution phase you start taking out $50,000 a year. If suddenly the market drops 20 percent for a couple of years running . . . you're going back to work. You no longer have enough invested to maintain that $50,000 a year income."

Hal and Margaret looked chagrined, but Keith smiled reassuringly. "Here's the solution," he said. "Say you're that person with a million dollars saved, and rather than putting it all in the market, you take $250,000 out to keep in a fixed 'bucket.' The remaining $750,000 you invest in the market. Over the next ten years, with a little help from Social Security and other savings, you live on that $250,000 and spend it to zero. You've just bought yourself ten years during which that $750,000 can really work for you. You've bought yourself time to rely on your investments averaging out."

Hal and Margaret silently processed this information for a moment.

"Basically what I'm saying," Keith explained, "is that taking out a somewhat larger chunk of cash to live on at the beginning of retirement and investing the rest could help protect your principal over time."

"This is incredible!" Hal said. "Why hasn't anyone told me this before?"

"Well, to be honest, it's more work for me to manage your money this way," Keith said simply. "It's easier for advisers to put all your money in one place, so this probably isn't their solution of choice."

"Of course," Hal said, the realization dawning on him. "But now that we know this, Margaret and I can be much more thoughtful about how we spend our money—and our time."

"Exactly," Keith agreed. "The next step for us from here is to break your income into 'buckets' so that you're not dealing with abstract sums of money but thinking about goals and purpose instead."

Keith pulled up Hal and Margaret's planning guide on the screen, and together they went back to the central question that Keith always started with: *What needs to happen in the next three years, personally and professionally, for you to feel happy and successful?**

Margaret wanted to continue volunteering at the children's hospital fifteen hours per week. She had been volunteering quite a bit there since her children had started college, and she had solid relationships with the doctors and nurses on staff. She felt that they had come to depend on her to help coordinate other volunteers, and the work itself was extremely rewarding. The doctors told her that families saw her as a calm, reassuring presence during some of their most frightening hours.

Margaret and Hal also wanted to consider purchasing a condo in the city where their daughter, Debra, lived. Their son, Alan, lived with his wife and two young children close to them, so they were able to see him and his family often. But they saw Debra and her new husband only on holidays or special occasions, and now that she was expecting her first child, they wanted to be able to spend more time with her. So purchasing a modest condo, and regularly purchasing plane tickets, was one of their most important buckets.

After Hal and Margaret had listed these items, they fell silent, not sure what else to tell Keith.

"Well, what about you, Hal?" Keith asked. "I asked you earlier, both personally and *professionally*, have you thought about the next three years? Is there an organization that you'd like to give time to on a regular basis, while Margaret's volunteering at the children's hospital?"

Hal paused. "You know, I've been thinking about it a lot," he said. "And I'm just not sure. I certainly have an unusual skill from my career as a public speaker, and it was something that I really loved doing. In fact, it's what got Richard and me started on this exploration in the first place. I was sitting out on the water on a fishing trip, and I suddenly said to myself, 'Fish don't clap.' I realized I missed my speaking engagements. But I'm having trouble thinking of how I can keep some part of that former life going in my retirement."

"Does it have to be your former life?" Keith asked. "You know, I've got a lot of clients who don't think of retirement as retirement; instead, they think of it as a time when they work *a lot less*. But they still keep that link to their career identity. I just spoke with a client this morning who was a partner at an extremely successful law firm. He's been retired six years, but he still does legal work for a pro bono client or two throughout the year. He's probably working only 10 percent as much as he used to, so he can still enjoy the fruits of his career. He and his wife are planning a trip to Japan later this year, in fact. But he gets a lot of personal fulfillment out of the fact that he still has a reason to read law review articles and go to bar meetings. At social events, he introduces himself as an attorney, rather than a retired attorney."

Both Hal and Margaret were completely absorbed

in Keith's story, and a little gleam was starting to appear in Hal's eye.

"Of course, this is entirely personal, and I'm not here to say that one way or another is the best way. I also have clients who worked long and hard during their careers, and now that they're retired, they want to stay that way. If they do any work at all, it's around the house or as volunteers in fields that have nothing to do with their past career. They earned their break, and they're enjoying it.

"And," Keith continued, "I have clients who don't want to be fully retired, but they don't necessarily want to keep doing exactly what they used to be doing. One of my clients has 'tuition' as one of her buckets—but not her children's tuition, *her* tuition, because she wants to go back to school for social work after she retires from managing a dental office."

Hal was smiling broadly. "I can't believe I never thought of it before," he said. "But you're right—there's no reason why I have to be either working full-time or be fully retired. There's a middle ground!" He turned to Margaret, his eyes sparkling with that entrepreneurial glint that she knew so well.

"I know exactly what I'm going to do," he said.

CHAPTER SEVEN

Putting it All Together

HAL SAT IN a corner booth at a café downtown on a Tuesday afternoon in early November. Through the window, he was starting to see foot traffic pick up on the sidewalks. The busy lunch hour was just beginning.

Hal watched as men and women in dark business clothes rushed past the window. Some were talking urgently on cell phones or earpieces. Some were clutching briefcases and easing their way through the crowd, heads bent. Occasionally a group of colleagues would pass, deep in conversation, gesturing as they walked.

Absentmindedly, Hal picked up a spoon and stirred his coffee, still gazing out the window. He could remember the feeling of a busy weekday lunch hour well—and almost to his surprise, it dawned on him that he didn't miss it. He was perfectly happy to be sitting down to a leisurely lunch as a retired person, with the afternoon open and unscheduled before him. A slow smile spread across his face.

Just then, a voice drew Hal out of his thoughts.

"Hal! I'm glad to see you!"

Hal looked up to see his friend Richard standing at the end of the booth, beaming. Richard was dressed in a grey business suit with navy tie slightly askew, a laptop bag slung loosely over his shoulder. He looked like he had materialized directly out of the crowd of professionals outside.

"Richard!" Hal exclaimed. "What a great surprise. I was just going to get some lunch. Do you want to join me?"

The two of them exchanged a hearty handshake, and Richard slid into the booth opposite Hal. He gave his watch a quick check.

"I can stay only about forty-five minutes," Richard explained. "I've got a meeting in the early afternoon."

"Then let's get you something to eat," Hal said warmly, passing Richard a menu. "You know, it's funny I ran into you today," he continued, as he and Richard began to look over the menu, "because I really need to thank you. I'm sitting here at this café today because of you."

Richard gave Hal a curious look. "How so?"

"Well," Hal said, "I came here to get a little work done because . . . I've accepted a speaking engagement. After we started talking at the lodge, it occurred to me for the first time that I don't have to completely remake who I am now that I'm retired. It's not like there's a Working Hal and a Retired Hal who are two separate people.

"I realized that my work as a public speaker meant more to me than just bringing in an income. It was an important part of my identity. And there are other parts of my identity that I want to focus on now, but that doesn't mean I have to forget that speaking is something that I love and I'm good at."

Richard was nodding enthusiastically. "So you're getting back out there?" he asked.

"Yes," Hal answered, tapping a notebook on the table between them. "Not full time. Maybe just one or two engagements a month. And the best part is . . . " He paused. "Well, actually, I think I'll let the best part be a surprise."

Richard was intrigued, but just as he was about to press Hal for more details, the server arrived. They ordered their sandwiches, and before Richard knew it, the conversation had moved on to other topics.

It had been several weeks since they'd last seen each other in passing at Keith's office, so they had a lot to catch up on. Richard told Hal about how his older son, Sam, was finishing up his last year of college and applying to a few prestigious business schools. His younger son, Peter, was still staying clean and was a well-liked and trusted employee at the record store where he worked.

Hal responded in kind with news about how he and Margaret would be spending Thanksgiving with their daughter. They had decided to spend an extra week with her so that they could look at condos in the city where she lived and consider purchasing one.

"I'm realizing that a couple of speaking engagements a month will be the perfect balance," Hal said. "Enough to keep me engaged and challenged—but not so much that I can't make my family my primary focus for this stage of my life. Realizing that I can strike this balance has made me feel genuinely grateful to be retired. Just before you came in, I was watching all the businesspeople outside rushing around on their lunch hour, and I realized that I wouldn't want to trade places. Retirement is starting to agree with me."

"Oh yeah?" Richard said. "I have to say, I wouldn't mind trading places. Today is one of those days at the office!" He laughed good-naturedly. "But seriously, Hal, that's great news. It's a far cry from where you were when we first met."

"It is," Hal agreed. "And I've got you and Keith to thank for it. It was that conversation we had at the lodge that really started the wheels turning for me. And then when we met Keith—that's when things really took off. I'm starting to feel a lot more at ease in my own skin again. Like I still have purpose, even if I'm not heading to work every day."

"That's fantastic," Richard said. "And I have to say, it sounds a lot like what's been happening for me and Alice ever since we started working with Keith. Granted, we're not quite in the same life stage as you and Margaret, but we're still starting to plan seriously for the future. And I'm feeling a lot better about where we are right now, now that I have a clear picture of where we're going and how we're going to get there."

Hal nodded. "I never would have thought a financial advisor's office would be the place to address the kinds of big life questions I was dealing with."

"Me neither," Richard agreed. "But it kind of makes sense, doesn't it? I'm starting to think of our family's financial plan as the hub that all our other plans stem out from. Keith helped us make sense of how our finances are right now and also how we want them to be in the future. From there, we were able to create plans for things like Sam's tuition and our vacation home and travel in the future."

"That's a great way of putting it," Hal said. "Keith helped us get organized so that we had a good sense of our financial life and the opportunities available to us, all in one place. In fact, he literally put everything all in one place. Did he help you get set up with his tracking software?"

"He did! It's an incredibly efficient system," Richard said.

Hal was referring to an online tool that Keith provided for his clients. Simply put, it was an application that could consolidate a family's entire financial life. With help from Keith's staff, Hal and Margaret had uploaded information from their bank accounts, credit cards, loans, and investments. The application was self-updating, so every night it synced information from all of their accounts. The result was a single location where Hal and Margaret could either find one number stating their net worth or break down their finances into minute detail, including checking account balances or projected investment income.

The tool was a simple and functional way for Keith to collaborate with clients on an ongoing basis. He didn't have access to all of the private budgeting information collected by the tool, but he could look up information for various investment accounts, such as IRAs and 401(k)s, and make sure he was staying ahead of important changes.

"What I really love about it," Hal said to Richard now, "is the online vault. Margaret and I are pretty good about saving all our important documents, but they're still not always easy to find when we want them. My file drawers are brimming with all kinds of papers—some of them important and some not. I used to cringe when I thought about something unexpected happening to me or Margaret. What if my kids needed to find our power of attorney or something like that quickly? They'd have to sift through all these irrelevant old bank statements and warranties and who knows what else before they found it.

"But Keith showed us how we could use the online tool to upload all of our important documents—our will, health care directives, even copies of our driver's licenses and passports. His staff helped us get all that stuff scanned, and now it's stored in one easy place."

The online tool provided different levels of permissions for different documents. So some documents could be private for Hal and Margaret only; others were viewable by their kids; and still others could be accessed by Keith or other professionals, such as their CPA or attorney.

"Margaret and I feel a lot more secure about traveling now, knowing that everything is so well organized online, and we can access anything we might need no matter where we are in the world."

Richard nodded enthusiastically. "You know," he said, "the thing I really like about the online tool is that it's helping Alice and me to budget. It tracks what we're spending each month and on what kinds of items or services. So we finally have a real-world report on how much we need for each of the different expenses in our lives. We were able to report back to Keith with that information, and that helped him create a realistic picture of how much we can save from our income.

"From there, he can use the tool to show us different future scenarios. Like what our retirement income might look like if the market averages 5 percent a year versus 7 percent, and so forth. It helps us review our 'buckets'—like Sam's tuition and paying down our vacation home mortgage."

Hal smiled ruefully. "I'll probably never be willing to spend enough time on the computer to really take advantage of those functions," he admitted. "Margaret and I still prefer the old-fashioned way most of the time. We've still got our quarterly statements coming in the mail and our face-to-face meetings with Keith, and that works just fine.

"Even setting the fancier technical capabilities aside," he said, "it really is a remarkable tool. It fits so neatly into the bigger picture of what Keith is trying to do for us. I'm sure he talked to you about gaps and solutions?"

"Absolutely," Hal said. "That's the backbone of the work Margaret and I are doing with him."

"Right," Richard agreed. "Keith helped Alice and me to identify gaps in our planning, and from there, over time, we're coming up with solutions to fill in those gaps. And one of the most eye-opening solutions he offered us was his concept of 'buckets.' Instead of just lumping all of our savings together, we divided it up into buckets—so that we know exactly how much we're saving for what kinds of future activities or purchases.

"The tracking software fits perfectly with that concept. Alice and I decided, for example, that we want to be setting money aside for European travel. So we can use the online tool to check on our progress with that bucket. And then when we actually *are* traveling, if we need access to documents—they're right there in the online tool! Keith has gotten us organized in a way we never were before."

"I'll say!" Hal agreed. "You know what's been most surprising to me about all this?"

"What's that?" Richard asked.

"It's not a hassle!" Hal exclaimed. "I think part of the reason that Margaret and I always did the minimum planning possible was just that all the paperwork and organization and finding the right professionals for the right tasks always seemed so daunting. We kept putting things off until the very last minute, which meant that our planning was always piecemeal. We waited to do a power of attorney until I was about to have a hernia surgery and we just couldn't ignore it any longer. And the only thing that made us consider putting a will together was the birth of our first grandchild. We waited on everything until life gave us a shove in the right direction. Because of that, we weren't planning as effectively as we could have been because we were being more reactive than proactive."

Richard nodded. "That's the mode Alice and I were in, too. Only we were much further behind than you and Margaret. We hadn't even started on most of the legal arrangements and insurance policies that Keith recommended for us to have in place. But just as you say, it actually hasn't been a hassle. Instead, it's been a relief to identify our gaps and to have Keith help us outline a manageable, step-by-step plan for implementing solutions over time. He also suggested a fairly innovative way for us to set up an inheritance plan for our sons."

Richard explained to Hal the plan for purchasing a life insurance policy to benefit Peter, so that he would receive assets comparable to those Sam would receive as the heir to Richard's company.

"It involves purchasing a life insurance policy, working with our attorney to draft a will and a trust, and communicating with our sons to make sure they understand the plan," Richard said. "It sounds like a lot of work, but Keith is functioning as the center point of this broader network of professionals. He's helping to coordinate the whole process. In the end, rather than feeling daunting, it feels good to know we're getting things taken care of."

"That's been my experience, too," Hal agreed. "We've done the same thing—instead of saying, 'Okay, here are all the gaps, let's try to take care of them all at the same time,' we outlined a slow process for taking care of the more urgent things first and then adding more solutions over time. It doesn't feel like a chore; it feels like necessary and reassuring preparation for our future."

Richard smiled. "If you had told me last summer that my solo hiking trip was actually the first step on a path toward a more secure financial future, I never would have believed it," he said. "But I'm really glad we ended up having that brainstorming session."

"You're telling me," Hal said. A little glint appeared in his eye. "And the benefits are only just starting to take shape for me. Are you free next Saturday morning? I'd like to invite you to my speaking engagement."

CHAPTER EIGHT

Value Above and Beyond the Ordinary

AS HAL DROVE home after lunch with Richard, he began to reflect on the journey he had been on over the previous few months. He had started by being astonished to discover that satisfaction and fulfillment weren't his automatic reward at the hard-earned end of a long career. Now he was beginning to formulate a plan for proactively creating the fulfillment he yearned for. As he had expressed to Richard, he was surprised to discover that some of the answers he had been seeking had come from financial planning.

Yet, it made sense. The work he was doing with Keith took his entire life into account. It was about envisioning the future and defining the steps necessary to make that vision real.

The word that Hal kept coming back to as he reflected was *value*. What Keith offered clients went far beyond simple investment advice. It provided real *value* that was creating change in Hal's life.

Keith approached the advising relationship in a fundamentally different way from many financial advisors. In the past, Hal had been used to seeing his financial advisors' roles as being fairly compartmentalized. They were responsible for investing his money and occasionally advising changes in response to the market. But they hadn't become involved in his process of setting goals and attaining them. If he and Margaret had specific financial goals, such as purchasing a home or taking a big trip, it had been up to them to decide how much they would need and when they would need it and to regulate their own decisions to get there. Sometimes they were successful, but often setting clear parameters for themselves had proven difficult for them. Financial strategizing just wasn't part of Hal's skill set.

From the beginning, the process had been different with Keith. And it was right there in the service agreement Hal and Margaret had signed when they'd decided to work with him. The first sentence was: "Our clients are partners." That was exactly the difference. Keith had become a true collaborator in Hal and Margaret's planning for a more fulfilling future.

The service agreement continued, "Together we have a single goal, and that is to reach your financial goals today and in retirement. As partners, we share this responsibility for success."

That perfectly encapsulated the role Keith was playing in helping Hal and Margaret map out the coming months and years. It wasn't that he was getting over-involved in elements of Hal and Margaret's life that they already had under control. Instead, he was helping them clarify hopes and ambitions that they had never been clear about before. Having their goals clearly stated made it possible to make a workable plan for achieving them—and because Keith saw himself as a partner, he was invested in helping Hal and Margaret stick to their plan.

That sense of investment wasn't abstract, either. It was actively reflected in Keith's compensation plan. All the advisors Hal had worked with in the past had charged for their services on a commission basis. That meant that if he had a hundred thousand dollars to invest, they would take the money and invest it, charging sometimes up to 5 percent as a front-end commission. From there, the performance of those investments didn't really make a difference to the advisors—they had already been paid. That was the traditional way of doing business through a broker, and it hadn't occurred to Hal that there was an alternative.

When Hal and Margaret had transferred their accounts to Keith's firm, they had agreed to pay him a yearly 1 percent management fee—with no up-front commissions. That meant that Keith's compensation was tied to the performance of the assets he was managing on Hal and Margaret's behalf. His fee would rise and fall as the value of their portfolio rose and fell. As Keith put it, this aligned his values with those of his clients. He was motivated to monitor investments and make wise decisions, because if he didn't, his net compensation would likely suffer.

Significantly, this also meant that he had no incentive to make arbitrary decisions. Keith explained to Hal that a large part of making wise investment decisions is not overreacting to market fluctuations. He told Hal about a study done by a major investment bank showing that over a twenty-year period, stocks averaged an 8 percent yearly increase and bonds averaged 6 percent. But the average investor holding those products tended to earn only about 2 percent per year. Why? Because they would react to the market and make changes in their investments rather than staying the course and trusting the average rates to even out in their favor over time.

Keith told Hal that a significant part of his job was helping to guide and direct investor behavior. "It's easy to be an advisor when the market is good," Keith said. "It's harder when the market is bad and the advice is, 'Just wait.'" But giving that advice had been his primary role during the downturn of 2008—and it had paid off for his clients.

Keith further explained that sometimes brokers were motivated by their commissions to make unnecessary or unadvisable changes in investments. Many can charge both a front-end and back-end commission by selling and buying stocks. But a family's investments are like a bar of soap—the more a broker plays with them, the smaller they get.

By contrast, Keith's compensation structure meant that he had the incentive to behave like a real partner in monitoring Hal and Margaret's investments. And the 1 percent management fee paid for far more than portfolio management. It also included all the services that went into coming up with a comprehensive financial plan for the couple—from helping them purchase the right kinds of insurance policies to helping them create a plan for passing on assets to their beneficiaries. That was value that Hal hadn't even imagined was possible in a financial advising relationship.

Keith had also talked very candidly with Hal and Margaret, explaining to them that meeting their goals would often mean paying attention to their spending and saving behaviors. Hal was grateful that Keith was willing to have tough conversations with them and to help them stick to their commitments. He had even given them a few examples of how he had interceded when he saw that clients were getting in the way of their own futures by overspending in the present.

One of Keith's clients was a corporate CPA working for a nationwide retail giant. The CPA made $400,000 a year, but he had a $250,000 mortgage on his home and another $100,000 mortgage on his vacation home. When he and his wife came to Keith with the idea of purchasing a third home, Keith gave them a very realistic look at the numbers. If they went ahead with the purchase, the husband would be working until he was 70 to pay off the mortgages. Then Keith asked them the real hard question: "You know right now that your company is doing okay, but are you confident it will continue to do well until you're 70? Are you positive that your job is secure?"

As a result of this conversation, the husband and wife had decided—prudently—that the third home wasn't actually aligned with their goals.

Another client came to Keith and told him that his job was simply too high stress and he wanted to retire at the age of sixty. Because Keith saw it as part of his job to help people match their finances with the rest of their lives, including staying healthy and fulfilled, he wanted to do his best to help this client retire early. But it meant a conscious readjusting of the family's plans.

Normally, Keith accounted for 3 percent inflation in helping clients plan retirement income. But because this client wanted to retire a full six years earlier than he had originally planned, he and Keith agreed to raise his income by only 1 percent each year so that it could stretch further. They were able to create a plan that would allow the client to maintain his income, with 1 percent yearly raises, until he was 93—but that was the year the money would run out. Keith very carefully went over the details of the plan with both the husband and wife and made sure that they understood the risks involved. Together they printed out a plan for the couple to sign off on. It was less than ideal, and Keith would have preferred a less risky solution, but through honest and open discussion, he and his clients had arrived at an agreement together—an agreement in which the clients understood that they were trading some degree of financial security for the mental and physical health benefits of earlier retirement.

Hal had been impressed with these stories. Keith was going far beyond the numbers and figures and taking the clients' whole selves—personal and professional—into account. Hal just had a gut feeling that Keith was a straight shooter. Sure, he had significant experience and skill, but there was something else there, something less tangible. It was clear to Hal that Keith cared deeply about creating a bright future for him and Margaret and that he would do what was best for them, no matter what.

Hal recalled Keith saying, "I operate by the golden rule of advising. I give my clients the advice I would want to get about my own money. That means that I'm straightforward about risks. I'm realistic about how far your money can stretch. And I don't put your money into any investments that I wouldn't purchase myself."

As Hal pulled into his driveway, looking forward to a relaxing afternoon at home with Margaret, he smiled to himself. The real value of working with Keith was that he would be providing clarity and confidence for the rest of both his and Margaret's lives.

CHAPTER NINE

Looking Ahead with Confidence

IT HAD BEEN a long time since Hal had been this nervous. He could hear his blood rushing in his ears and his heart knocking against his rib cage. Yet, there was something almost pleasant about this nervousness. It felt familiar. It felt like home.

It was the morning of Hal's return to the speaking circuit. He had gone over his notes and was feeling prepared. In fact, he felt more than prepared—he felt *energized*. He felt like he was returning to his life's purpose. He had taken the smallest seed of an idea that Keith had planted in his mind, and with a little tending, it had grown.

For Hal, today was more than simply having something to do in retirement. It was about more than enjoying the electricity of being in front of a crowd. Hal couldn't wait to get in front of the audience because now, possibly more than ever before, he had something to say.

Just then, a low rumble of applause spread over the audience as Hal heard himself being introduced by the conference host. For a microsecond, Hal hesitated. This was it. The sound—and the feeling—that had been missing when he was out on his fishing boat, surrounded by silence.

Fish don't clap, Hal thought, *but now I'm back*. He took a deep breath and stepped out onto a wide, brightly lit stage.

As he made his way to the podium, Hal beamed out at the audience and took in the sound of the applause. In the front row he could see his wife Margaret smiling up at him, and beside her sat his new friends Richard and Alice.

Hal stepped to the microphone.

"You've come here today because you're getting ready for retirement," Hal said, the microphone amplifying his voice for the assembled crowd of several hundred people. "This is a conference on everything you need to consider as you transition out of your career. You've attended seminars on everything from organizing your finances to choosing travel destinations. But now I want you to pause a moment and take a step back."

Hal allowed a brief silence to hang over the crowd.

"Have you asked yourself *why* you want to retire? You know what you're retiring *from*—a long and successful career, from which you've earned a break. But do you know what you're retiring *to*?"

Again, Hal paused. He was just hitting his stride. It was these "ah-ha" moments that he loved so much about speaking—the moments when he got a crowd to stop and think about things from a new perspective.

"When you're no longer able to define yourself by your job title or your profession . . . who will you be? How are you going to continue to be fulfilled by life and engaged in it? Retirement is both the end of a career and the beginning of a new phase of life—but all too often, the ending is what we wind up getting stuck on. We're caught off guard by feelings of loss, like we're suddenly unmoored and adrift without our professional identities.

"It's time to replace those feelings of loss with feelings of excitement about our newfound freedom. It's time to go from 'Now what?' to 'Anything is possible!' That's what I want to work with you on today."

Hal smiled out at the audience, briefly letting his eyes travel to his wife and friends in the front row. He knew he was exactly where he needed to be.

Planning for a Purposeful Retirement

CPSIA information can be obtained at www.ICGtesting.com
Printed in the USA
BVOW03s1400230415

397227BV00009B/348/P

9 780692 322741